Rainbow of Clouds

Rainbow of Clouds

Kamala Prasad Mahapatra

BLACK EAGLE BOOKS
Dublin, USA | Bhubaneswar, INDIA

 BLACK EAGLE BOOKS

USA address:
7464 Wisdom Lane
Dublin, OH 43016

India address:
E/312, Trident Galaxy, Kalinga Nagar,
Bhubaneswar-751003, Odisha, India

E-mail: info@blackeaglebooks.org
Website: www.blackeaglebooks.org

First International Edition Published by
BLACK EAGLE BOOKS, 2025

RAINBOW OF CLOUDS
by Dr. Kamala Prasad Mahapatra

Copyright © **Dr. Kamala Prasad Mahapatra**

All rights reserved. No part of this publication may be reproduced, stored in a retrieval system, or transmitted, in any form or by any means, electronic, mechanical, photocopying, recording or otherwise without the prior permission of the publisher.

Cover & Interior Design: Ezy's Publication

ISBN- 978-1-64560-761-8 (Paperback)

Printed in the United States of America

Dedication

Dedicated at the lotus feet of Parameswar,
Karuna avatar, Mahadeva, Mahakala, Asutosh,
Bhagawan Shiv Shankar.

Karpura Gauram Karunavataram
Sansara Saram Bhujagendra haram
Sada Basantam Hrudayaravinde
Bhavam Bhavani Sahitam Namami
OM Namoh Shivaya
Maha Rudraya.

Preface

Purnamadah purnamidam purnat purna mudachyate

Purnasya purnamadaya purnameva vasisyate .

We all know that poetry is one of the most significant and paramount genres of literature. It is believed that Poetry infuses life, enthusiasm, vibrancy, and resilience into the soul. Poetry is also considered as a dialogue between the soul and the silence that surrounds it.

William Wordsworth defined Poetry as a spontaneous overflow of powerful feelings recollected in tranquillity . Matthew Arnold defined that poetry is the criticism of life. T.S. Eliot defined poetry is not the turning loose of emotion but an escape from emotion, it is not the expression of personality but an escape from personality.

The essence of these three selective definitions, I believe, is reflected in the Poetry Collection "The Rainbow of Clouds". Poetry largely depends on poetic devices such as simile, metaphor, images and objective correlatives. The poet prefers to express his feelings, emotions and passions through poetic devices.

In this connection Wordsworth's views on poetic diction or language of poetry appear quite relevant. In "The Preface to Lyrical Ballads", Wordsworth defines Poetic Diction as follows: The poet should choose incidents and situations from ordinary and common life and throw a colour of imagination in such a manner so as to make ordinary things appear extraordinary and common things appear uncommon. The poet should use simple and colloquial language in poetry.

A very common issue is debated quite often in intellectual parlance that what do we call a poet, an ordinary man or extraordinary man. The answer, I believe is very simple and unanimous. The poet is of course an ordinary mortal with some extraordinary organic sensibility. When he observes an object, a sight, an incident all his five senses viz- touch, taste, smell, sight, hearing used to work in tandem to constitute his poetic vision, manifest his poetic oeuvre for creative work.

For example a tree may be described as a green cathedral with leaves whispering prayers to the wind. A temple may be described as a vessel of light floating on the tide of faith. A mountain may be described as a colossal monk draped in mist and meditation.

Poetry always serves the twin purpose of offering entertainment through aesthetic delight, blissful emotional portrayal and at the same time emitting the glow of enlightenment, intellectual discourse, moral, cultural concerns focusing on socio-political issues.

This Poetry Collection "The Rainbow of Clouds" contains the poems reflecting the desire to understand the fragments of human experience that embody the love, loss, emotion, passion, aberration, feeling, sentiment, faith, doubt, time, transition, hope, anxiety, agony, anguish and many more.

The poems in this Poetry Collection do not claim to resolve life's dilemmas but listen to them intently and depict the intangible elements such as fleeting emotion, sudden illumination, spiritual bliss, resilience that help wriggle out of the whirlpool of crisis and return to the mainstream.

If the poems resonate with the readers and cause ripples in their hearts I will feel satisfied that my labour is rewarded.

Finally I would like to offer my heartfelt thanks to my wife Baijayanti, mother Hiranyamoyee, daughters Mousumi, Monalisa, sons in law Badri Narayan, Ambika Prasad, son BibhuPrasad, daughter in law Dipanjyoti, grand childrenRitu, Riya, Piyu, Kuhu, Putul, Lubul for their motivation for this creative journey.

I would also like to extend my deep sense of gratitude to M/S Raju Graphics for typing the manuscript flawlessly and M/S Black Eagle Books , especially MrSatyaPatnaik and Mr Ashok Parida for their hard labour and commitment to bring out the book in time.

I also acknowledge the unwavering support and encouragement of my readers, friends and well wishers for which the book could see the light of the day.

Sarve bhavantu sukhina sarvesantu niramaya

Sarve bhadrani pasyantu maa kaschit dukha bhag bhavet.

Om shanti, shanti, shanti.

     Jay Jagannath.

Kamala Prasad Mahapatra

CONTENTS

Disturbing Memory	13
Pervading Anarchy	15
Receding Serenity	18
Where shall I settle	20
Day Break	22
Deliverance	24
Don't ask me	27
Nuptial Blessing	29
India : My Pride	32
The Achiever	34
Regret	37
Glider	40
Moonlit Night	42
Who is afraid?	45
A Fleeting Glimpse	47
Night of Rains	49
Life's Vagaries	51
Paperboat	53
Time Matters	55
Memory	56
Pangs	58
Sisyphean Strife	61
Inaccessible	63

How I Wonder	65
Welcome Blithe Newcomer	67
Balm	69
Frenzy Every where	71
After you Left	73
How I crave for	75
Warm Welcome	77
Gala Time	78
Whither Poetry	80
Somersault	82
Forlorn House	84
Mother Land	87
Open Vault Pandora's	90
Smooth Passage	93
In the Abyss	95
Mood swing	98
Phantom Unsalvageable	101
Not a Human indeed	103
Till the End	105
No Escape	107
Sylvan Dream	109
Not for Sharing	111
What was Feared	113
Meaningful Sojourn	115
Fly wings Fly	117
Siren	119
Deep Dive	121
River Daya's Saga	123

Disturbing Memory

Mere sojourn
short association
leave indelible impact
with insignia of
amazing experience
when such nostalgia
is razed into rubbles
it is difficult to
survey its longitude
and latitude
I only gaze at my orbit
in a daze
like a tsunami victim
surviving sudden fury

Very often your memory
Pops up dotes,
dances like
the blushing maiden cloud
clinging to the sky's chart
sometimes your memory
inspires,enthrals
stirs me like

the distant
yellow mustard field
lazying around
in a relaxed mood
your memory worries me
like the musk deer
looking for aroma around
little knowing
the source
enshrined
in her own navel.

Pervading Anarchy

Very often the dazed silence around
like that of crematorium
rattles us, makes us debate
on the source of it

silence is wrought
out of the aftermath
of tornado
unleashing deluge
of mundane woes

hooting of owls
overshadows
consecrated temple bells
Garden of Eden
is desecrated
forbidden fruit plucked
zealously gulped
at Satan's instigation
inviting corporeal
punishment of being
thrown out
from domain of innocence

esoteric ambience to splash
the space of bliss with bitterness
the dangling fruit from
tree of knowledge
with good and evil
lured Eve
to prevail on Adam
to pluck and taste.

birth of first sibling
Cain soaking earth
with Abel's blood
driven by envy,
hatred, revenge
unfolded
Pandora's box of sin

good, evil,
virtue, vice,
piety,sin
exist side by side
sin overpowers piety

carnage by terrorists
turn blissful innocence
into turbulence
Harish Chandra performs
Rohitashwa's funeral
Sabya is awestruck
a helpless spectator

Gandhi's concept of
truth nonviolence
fraternity peace harmony

blatantly ignored
limiting it
to birth anniversary
vague promises
holiday observance
routine garlanding of
abandoned morose statue
political chicanery
election rhetorics
resonate all around
mining slurs
chit fund scams
spreading octopus arms
brazenly ridicule
welfare state slogan
as myth euphemism veneer
to cross the river of election
riding on the boat
of hypocrisy and opportunism.

Receding Serenity

Within the bonejoints
among the blood platelets
on upper skin layer
in breath of nostrils
fresh but
quiet pain is palpable
subconscious agony
shoots pressure of blood

In hind sight
to others
it looks
a normal village
dotted with panorama
of picturesque landscapes
echoing avian warble
humming of bees
cooing of cuckoo
crooning of dove

view from a distance
makes me nostalgic
to hark back
to reminisce
dive in to and
soak in the

labyrinth of memory
to slowly retrieve
certain vignettes of past
incredible occasions
in present context
as it were

how festivals in past
were an amazing
source of wild ecstasy
sweet camaraderie
harbinger of harmony

Nature's vagaries
onslaughts fury
occasional floods famines
rains landslides
hailstorms
never dampen intensity
of emotions
rather are taken
in normal strides

phantom of misfortune
haunted trampled,
sautéed it since
globalization urbanization
spread their tentacles
crushed peace fraternity
harmony serenity
of village life
under the unrelenting
wheels of juggernaut.

Where shall I settle

Where shall I get
Walden pond
to settle nearby

there must be
pure sanctified water
to cleanse my soul
consecrate my body

before setting out
making the journey
upward, heavenward

I shall settle down
at a place where
there is
open azure sky
over head
murmuring sound
of fountain
abounding in
my near relations

hazy reminiscences
popping up
like head of
electronic doll
amid glimmer of anxiety

each moment shall
flicker with words
like flowers blooming
from buds every morning

humming of bees
dancing of peacocks
jumping of agile deer
shall be amazing
enriching, accomplishing

far away from
the gnawing
jaws of death
threatening
brandishing
deadly horns,
ghastly face
sitting on buffalo back.

Day Break

Crimson red colour
of setting sun
reflects its
pent up anger
after exerting
for the whole day
sweating panting
gasping
unwinding
chilling out
like a fitness freak
doing it at gym

every end
has beginning
it is said
if sun is not set
it cannot rise next day

leaving the carcass
to maggots
keeping
creation cycle aloft
golden rays
of morning sun

instill supple
soothing solace
leading
lotus petals unfold

like a cricketer
emerging after
scoring century
exuding confidence
and motivating peers

dew drops
on grass carpet
get reflected
to glisten like
silver particles
adding lustre to
cosy diurnal ambience
with soulful
avian melody

every rising sun
unleashes
promises galore
fills hearts
with fun, frolic
to fill its
resurgent vivacity
once more
after day break.

Deliverance

Flying aimlessly
in the sprawling sky
from east to west
up to the horizon
and again
diving down

the sportive bird
appears as it were
to gauge the
blue of the sky
coolness around
with eyes
full of dreams

the playful bird
flies up and up
in the morning sky
makes suitable sojourn
returns tired

groping under
the shadows of
hazy twilight

seeking any familiar
or unfamiliar trace
unhesitantly as its haven
like a rudderless ship
drifting in the sea
exploring looking
for harbor
for coincidental sojourn
unaware of
schedule of time
for heading
towards destination
hopes to spend the night
overcome the fatigue
of flying the whole day

flying indiscriminately
over cornfields
dark clouds,
mountains fountains
looks different
losing previous
zest agility
resilience and dream

like an aeroplane
looking for
safe landing
at an airport
with green signal

It is scared
to stumble against
any invisible object

and fall into
the sea or river

craves to be in the flock
and rest for the night
in exclusive nest

no matter if
it is nest of lotus petals
or cage of twigs

full day of freedom
makes the bird realise
that deliverance is
only possible
through detachment.

Don't ask me

Don't ask me
with what
apparently
rosy but
broken dreams
the foundation of
my empty villa is made

surrounded by flowers
bloomed from
agonies and anguishes
man lives
seething incessantly
sometimes voluntarily
or often under compulsion
trying to compromise but
not to hurt others

his hopes aspirations
plunge into fire of pursuit
like the helpless gnat
battles with death
as promoter of euthanasia

others praise him copiously
that dissolves
faster than time
little wondering to know
how painful moments
were evolved

he too is silent
as a saint speechless
as though since long
fate of the people
is like that mystery

which is to find a place
in others' hearts
for which they
deem their thoughts
as luck and share
joy with others.

Nuptial Blessing

Lord said ....
let there be light
and there was light
the mythical
Great chain of Being
offers Man
status next to God
Man is bestowed with
 power of judgment
to distinguish between
right and wrong

Man has the
divine qualities
the absolute
the infinite qualities,
the Brahman
of which
Atman is a part

three attributes
monitor streamline
Man's nature
sattwa tama raja
determine Man's conduct

ours is a country
that vouches for secularism
prioritizes humanism
on this coveted occasion
I have no qualms to say
marriages are made
 in heaven
 celebrated on Earth

marriage
apart from rituals
brings together
two hearts two minds
unites two souls

leads kindly light
in conjugal journey
Instills confidence
to overcome challenges

nevertheless
inevitable always happens
we are here
to lend legitimacy
recognition
to the emotional proximity
of two young minds
we are moved
impressed overwhelmed
to see
amazing chemistry
manifested between them
over the last few hours

the modesty sobriety
soft spoken nature
of the groom impels us
to gladly extend
our blissful approval

Bhagavad Gita speaks of
"Karmanya badhikarasthe
maaphalesukadachana"
christianity believes in
"God's rule shall prevail
in everything"

all religions
declare loudly
clearly emphatically
that God is
the prime mover
his will shall prevail
man is just an agent
to execute
the will of
the Almighty

once again
we express
our happiness
and gratitude
to the Almighty
praying for their
blissful conjugal life.

India : My Pride

India oh my India
scenic serene
sublime India
sylvan mountains
murmuring fountains,
pastoral backdrop
amazing flora and fauna

incredible India
vigilant India
against enemy incursion
enviable India
practicing principles
religious integration
secularism, tolerance
through Sanatan dharma
propagating
"Vasudhaiva Kutumbakam"

Showcasing
largest democracy
divergent rituals
customs tradition
festivals celebrations

doing wonders
as welfare state
in field of
agriculture, industry
science technology
to guard borders
achieve excellence
in education health
drawing road map
for prosperous India

I love my India
incredible India
unique India,
unparalleled India
let's all chant
in unison
Jay Bharat Jay Hind.

The Achiever

Grave is certainly
not the goal of life
cynics say
life is an empty dream
optimists view otherwise
electronic companies
launch huge
marketing campaign
lure customers
imbibe robust optimism
explore new avenues
to challenge
to shut down
the critics the cynics

to blow
the trumpet of success
amid unprecedented fanfare
gaiety enthusiasm
revelry festivity
motivation effervescence
excitement ecstasy
to signify
life is real
life is earnest

hope teaches
to join the strife
as a hero
in the bivouac of life
to achieve
the solemn aim
to withstand
the onslaughts
valiantly
beat the challenges
that pop up

no longer life is
hard to live
globalization ushered
new horizon
of hope,
made life
worth living

multi nationals made
amazon entry
laid out
myriad products
with aesthetic finish
affordable price
adorable performance

hassle free gadgets
heartthrob
of housewives

fridge AC water filter
micro wave TV
cater to
smallest human needs

mobile laptop music system
keep connected
with rest of the world
instills confidence
makes accomplished
householder
kudos to ajatasatru
for amazing charisma
the gigantic
stature makes
others feel wary
turn pale
drives lilliputs
into oblivion
this paean
is indeed
well deserved.

Regret

Moon is not yet pale
though autumn has left
winter is yet to set in

post autumn scenario
makes fog melt in shame
to shower
sprinkle on earth
unique Dusserah
festival is ushered in
with the arrival of
invincible Goddess
Maa Durga
symbolizing
victory of piety
over sin
embodying
mercy, justice

Kumara purnima
unleashes
aura of revelry
with seductive

full moon
germinating love
in the maidens' hearts

Gajalaxmi festival
soaked in
bounteous devotion
enables devotees
to be blessed with
bumper income
festival of
lights unfolding
good luck
aplomb enthusiasm

expectations galore
permeated with
glamour of
glowing diyas
seemed as it were
to inundate the world
with light of joy
drive out
dark clouds of sin
causing sorrow

Surreptitious thief
of time
steals joy
perpetrates sorrow
transient though
like lightening spark

joy and sorrow
birth and death
movement of seasons
are usual go of the world

festive ambience
disappears unnoticed
amid flow
of excitement
causing regret
wishing for
those blissful days
for a little longer.

Glider

Rattled by
materialism
illusoriness
hypocrisy

the phantom
of my past
pops up like
the magic toy's
face of moustachioed king

I fall back
on my loads
of memory sacks
and open them
like Pandora's box

reinvent my talent
hither to kept at bay
from public eye
and my own
hawk's eye
that could
paint Mona Lisa
as Leonardo Vinci

portray Cleopatra's
two faces
as Shakespeare
to entice
disillusion
countless
Caesars Antonys
refuting the clamour

stop women harassment
bring legislation
empower them

little knowing
about women's
inherent potential
no legislation
did empower
Goddess Durga
to maul Mahisasura ,
save the universe.

Moonlit Night

The moonlit night
unleashes
excitement galore
cautiously
guarded
by stray patches
of floating clouds

that appear
as it were
to lift the sky
like Lord Krishna
lifting Giri Govardhan
on his finger tip.

the clouds hovering
and scouting
across the sky line
are trusted sentinels
vested with
ensuring safety
across the boundary
of moonlight

trees and shrubbery
touch the horizon
standing silently
like a mischievous
school kid
sensing punishment

sylvan moon
with her supple shine
sneaks through leaves
fountains water
rivers waves

intriguing smile
of Mona Lisa
vast stretches
of corn fields
glitter at a distance
covered with a net of
thin fog layer

prying eyes
of moonlight
fall indiscriminately
on the sweet face of
a romantic beloved
dabbling in
domain of love

a jilted lover
ponderous
pensive frustrated
groping in
blind alley

to wriggle out
like a misled soldier
in a tunnel

the guile scorn
and contempt
can not be concealed

moonlight of truth
shall reveal them
like Columbus or Newton.

Who is afraid?

As an ordinary mortal
I am not
afraid of
cacophonous melee
of the buffalo rider
ghastly visage
deafening roar of
the ominous fleet

stay away stay away
silky glistening contours
of immortal streak
imbibes in me
indomitable courage
amazing confidence \
to take on
impending challenges

life as such for me
is a whirl pool
of challenges
in the eternally
revolving wheel
like sunshine
causing full moon
or new moon

earth moving ahead
causing lunar eclipse
obstructing
sun's glow to
fall on moon

the mammoth fleet
deafening sound of knell
marks the transition
from the terrestrial
to the ethereal

ushers in a mindset
to bid adieu to
youthful resilience
sizzling romance
chivalrous deeds

allow them to exit
like dews of winter morning
disappearing
after sunrise
make preparations
to welcome
spread out
the red carpet
for the spring
of salvation
is at the door.

A Fleeting Glimpse

On the snow-white
canvass of
moonlit night
dotted with stars
like diamonds
on gold bangles
when the church
appears to lift the
conspiring
stray clouds
like Lord Krishna
doing to Govardhan

I descend down
as an artist
to make a portrait
of my past
of my dreams
unrequited jilted

such rights in the past
disillusioned me
snatched hopes
dashed my ambitions
shattered my dreams

only the fleeting glimpses
thrilled me intermittently
anyone in my place
would have
behaved cynically

but never did I relent
behaved like
legendary Santiago
showing tenacity
of purpose
pursued the goal
apparently evasive
with unflinching devotion
and never-say-die spirit
to land up here
where I am now.

Night of Rains

It rains in torrents
throughout the night
no respite
the asbestos roof
echoes with
sabre rattling of war

from a distance
is visible
the shadow of
mythical Yama Raj
alighting from
buffalo back

thick pitch dark night
scares me
intermittent lightning
followed by thunder
rustling and creaking
sound of trees
speed up heart beat

after lashing out
for quite sometime

and cooling down
the heat of earth

bestowing new
lease of life
on bushes,
shrubs, humans
creates an
aura of dream

weaves a boutique of
makebelieve world
like the rudderless
aimless dark
floating clouds
popping up
from sky's lap

dreams of
Kajol Roy and
Payal Sharma
haunt me
intensely like
never before.

Life's Vagaries

Can anyone tell
what is this life?
this life friends
is really funny
you agree or not

I feel it is
unpredictable
mysterious
unintelligible
inscrutable

like the floating clouds
in August sky
not very certain
of its own itinerary
tossed helter and swelter
by the whimsical wind

capricious fate
plays pranks
at our cost
makes us laugh

and yet upsets
the applecart
inducing agony

fledgling boat of life
strives amid ups
as well as downs
like a convict
eagerously awaiting
for royal clemency.

Paper boat

You love to make paper boats
on the pages of
my love's confession
I know it for certain
the ripples of resilience
speak volumes
through your face

your silence is infectious
the octopus grip captures
dabbles fondles my emotions
your amorous dalliance
subtle winks of passion
stare anxiously

stir my heart's citadel
no less than
a horrendous hurricane
severe tsumami
as it were
paper boats
float unhindered
in the water
of your secret passion

your bastion of love
is dedicated to me
I know it for sure
your secretive move
perpetuates monopoly

your usual broadness
shrinks apparently
to counter aliens
your selfish monopoly
your unabashed
claim on me
is simply swayed
on the paper boat
amid the sizzling chill
of flowing water

bumpy journey
of paper boat
flowing fragrance
of flowers
redolent breeze
softly caresses
my wounded passions
blows me away
into the paper boat
of your love
away and away
from cares anxieties.

Time Matters

Muscles of memory
tensed hard
rusted junked
abandoned
nudge me sizzle me

Time is what
always matters
even if past

faded although
volunteers to mentor
as the beacon to a sailor
amid the storm at night

Tiresias can foresee
Phoenician sailor's death
it's a veiled warning
Kuru clan decimation
offers wisdom galore

never ever unleash
obstinate arrogance
shed envy hatred
be kind humane
just get tucked
in pristine logo
Vasudhaiva Kutumbakam.

Memory

Memory hangs
in the eye's corner
as incessant
September rain drops
often it settles
under the red lips
with colours
of spring
to release
peals of laugh

mind's Yamuna flows
brings thrill
of gulmohar
shakes heat
with flute's symphony

memory often
is a silver moon

that pops up
as a snap in twilight
may be with
supple suave touch
of jasmine
or sweet nudge of rose

memory is
an unforgettable lyric
that oozes emotion
to float like
an aimless boat
in the flowing river
not to return ever.

Pangs

Swathed in prenatal
pool of saliva
the foetus seethes
in labour pain
shrieks and squirms
impatiently
in its bid
to wriggle out
to have a
glimpse of the dawn

It has so long been a myth
like Dharmapada's
immolation, sacrifice
a plunge into the sea
after setting
the crowning slab
of Konark temple
thus saving
the self esteem
of twelve thousand artisans

reeling under
labour pangs
groping in the gloom

of maternal womb;
the baby cries out
unleashing
a wave of enthusiasm
filling the arena
with new hopes
buoyancy and resilience

as the spring unfolds
a spirit of fun and revelry
ushering the 'Holi'
the festival of colours
bestowing
new blossoms
upon the trees

gala birthday bash
hails the baby as 'Messiah'
congratulations wishes
pour in
from myriad quarters
inaundate him
like freak summer rains

will the cheers last?
or dissolve like
bubble... like life?
who knows?
not anyone really
but alas !
the mythical light
the apocalypse of dawn
hardly promises anything

baby groans
in penitential anguish
like the 'Magi'
in midway
gloats over
the abject indifference
of people

galloping decadence
hurts him
turns him to 'Belalsen'
the golden bird
of Byzantium
to record it
on the springboard
of time
like Philomela sings
her woeful song

behaves chandrasena's way
to countdown
the doomasday
of Yadav clan
pave the way
for 'Ekalavya's chivalry.

Sisyphean Strife

The line of demarcation
between nectar and poison
gadually tapers to become
indistinct, nonexistent
once life takes shape
 tossing the baby
out of the
anaesthetic abyss

tied up with
Sisyphean predicament
grows up
little knowing
the grievous consequence
plays gleefully
hide and seek
with death, the tormentor
apparent liberator

like a vehicle in
undulating bumpy terrain
like an aircraft in
overcast hazy sky
begins the roller coaster journey

resolves firmly to withstand
the onslaughts of tsunami
refuses to be blown away
by hurricane of sufferings

he realizes pretty well
a valiant fighter
deserves kudos
trickling from
the aroma of
heartrending sighs
from the
impeccably carved
immortal portraits
preserved in the
glittering
golden chest of time

life is steeped
in eternal struggle
intermittently
defying death
vindicating
own supremacy.

Inaccessible

When I am affected by
octopus of materialism
confidence looks pale
like moon
under Rahu's spell

I look for opportunity
in anxiety
like September sky's sun
playing hide and seek
with floating clouds
to escape from
vicious circle

I am Abhimanyu
of mother's womb know
to sneak into
formidable
vicious circle
but ignorant
to wriggle out of trap

burden ridden upset self
pushes pandora's box
of thoughts

phantom of my past
pops up like
moustachioed
monarch's head
of magic toy

I wonder
why did
learned charioteers
weave vicious circle

why do politicians
make many dalits
pawn of their dice

why is there
incidence of rape of women
sexual harassment

beware Dushasans
Mahisasuras
there may be yet
Yajnaseni, Durga
to maul you
to rid the world
of heinous crimes.

How I Wonder

I really wonder
how you emerge
from long forgotten
remote past
which I had
thrown off
like a fly
from the milk bowl.

It's intriguing indeed
you evolve from
vales forests
mountains
springs of uncertainty
hazy horizons
of unrelenting memory
mixing it
with desire
stirring dull veins
with spring rains
of romance

corpse of memory
was laid into coffin
of alienation

buried in debris
of crematorium
to avoid
phoenix like appearance

fate of such happenings
is like the
morning dews
hanging on
the boughs of
soft lush green grass
or the fledgling baby bird
acquiring flying skill
with curiosity
to chart its
aeriel course
in sprawling skyline.

Welcome Blithe Newcomer

Tumult of calamities
shook the edifice of society
rich and poor
bruised and battered
expectant mother
thrilled but disturbed
by hope and expectation
about child's safety

it's obvious
which mother
is not concerned
about her child's future
given the background
of catastrophe unforeseen

days of anxiety
come to an end
labour pain ends
baby emerges
from the pool

of prenatal fluid
jumps like a playful calf
from eastern horizon

fills the surrounding
with uncanny glow
peeps into
the dew soaked
window panes
with crimson red
soft soothing rays

propagates the message
loud and clear
wait and watch
nothing is lost
nothing is irretrievable

joys follow sorrows
spring follows winter
corpse of outgoing year
shall pave the way
for building the
pyramid of New year
generating new hopes
unlimited bliss and plenitude.

Balm

Monthlong
hibernation
causes concern
where are you ?
if we think of you
remember you
why can't you respond ?

our sweet little
cute cuckoo
life is dull
loses charm
in your absence
anxiety to have
your proximity
enjoy mesmerizing
melodious cadence
is beyond control

your clamorous demand
arouses envy
in any sentient being
having a bit of
aesthetic sense

cuckoo's freedom
unfettered whims
to do and act
as per own choice

speak volumes
on human condition
helpless desperate
kept under
divine restraint
supreme hindrance

the bird is born perhaps free
man is in chains every where
I ask myself
how come the bird
is unfettered
Man, a superior animal
holding respectable position
in the hierarchy
of great chain of being
works under duress
dipped in
cares anxieties
torn by trials
and tribulations
only puts up pretence
of regulating everything

cuckoo appears as
blithe newcomer
during spring
to entertain the
morose human race
through its
scintillating melody
by anointing
the balm
of eternal anodyne.

Frenzy Every where

For some days now
there is frenzy every where
wheel of vicious circle
spreads tentacles
frenzy is unsparing
our hard earned freedom
prevailingdemocracy
are all victims of frenzy

there is no place
for reasoning
they say eccentricity
greed avarice hysteria
become household names

popular speeches
book launching ceremonies
project inauguration
populist welfare programmes
bear imprints of frenzy

frenzied paranoids
and carnivores
are perhaps identical
work in tandem
self-interest is motto

they swallow every thing
blame insult contempt
including bundles of
currency notes

quintals of fake ethics
ride roughshod
to achieve narrow
political end
without caring
for the means
like an examinee
keeping the end
of brilliant result
in view
aspires to
score high marks
through unfair means.

■

After you Left

After you left
I am rattled and upset
it feels good
to walk alone
on the quiet path
watching your beauty
on the swings of wind
listening to
your lilting words
amid the rustling of leaves
and cacophony of birds

After you left
Time is hanging heavy
head carries
burden of emptiness
mind is trapped
by deep gloom
hot respiration of hiatus
puts off the lamp of wisdom

after you left
loneliness envelopes
noon of youth

meets twilight
senility peeps in

I crave for peace
and deliverance
groping amid
thick pitch darkness

pearl of luminous flame
never emerges
from ocean's foliage

after you left
I gaze at the
distant horizon

azure sky
touches my
yearning heart
in the distant
enigma of
dream world .

How I crave for

How I crave for
getting your company
your sweet smile
slanting, mischievous looks

sitting close to each other
never ending
humour and jokes
in social circle

your mild rebuke
disdainful pretence
my allegorical description
of your dusky body
all have
a mesmerizing impact

you turn into
a colourful butter fly
by the magic touch
of my finger

I know not
if you relish it
but sweet rhythms
emerge from
your crimson lips

love flows like
sundry youthful dreams
illusory contentment of
first attachment
causes nostalgia

the rudderless waves of
busy schedule
the calm proximity
of the harbour
together combine
to produce sweet rhythm
instill positive assurance
promise fruition

the mercantile ship
exits hesitantly
not being sure
about tomorrow's return
with new merchandise

tomorrow's sun
shall bring new colours
play hide and seek
with its shadow as usual

song of love
thrills today
keeping tune with it
I sing daily
songs of ecstasy
without bothering
for tomorrow.

Warm Welcome

Turning aside the
tumult and turbulence
of the cataclysmic cyclone
the boisterous torrent of yuletide
and tsunami of new year wishes
inaundate the shaken edifice
of times, floor of hearts
fog soaked windowpanes
bringing a handful of relief
reassurance of flourish
whole world is agog

to welcome and embrace
the newborn baby
jumping gleefully
from the lap of
the crimson horizon

Showering tons of solace
this shall never be
a repeat of the past
with a firm resolve
to build the
pyramid of love and bliss
on the carcass of the past.

Gala Time

Spring recedes
keeping pace
with cycle of seasons
gyrating eternally
overriding interruptions
unfazed by convulsions
thrilling breeze
cuckoo's throbbing melody
are things of past
scorching summer
alights with heat humidity
throwing life out of gear
parching under sizzling heat
tormented by grueling humidity
people look for breather
in torrents of rain drops

denuded shrubs
get new lease of life
hopes germinate
generate new thrill
rains usher in
Rajo festival

an agrarian festival
of revelry galore
amazing reunion

unwed village maids
with throbbing sensation
enjoy festival to the hilt
with betel, baked cake
mutton and swings

farmers relax
stop cultivation
provide rest
to menstruating earth

after three days
earth is ready
to conceive embryo
like a woman
becoming ready
for pregnancy
after menstrual cycle

rain soaked earth
emits sweet aroma
after long hiatus
of cruel Summer
unwed village dames
drift their sweet dreams
like clouds in sky

stretch their dreams
to the heights and length
covered by the swig
hoping dreams to soon
turn into reality.

Whither Poetry

Driven by the muse
like the wind
driving dry leaf
struck by the labour pain
like on expectant mother
to deliver the babe,
under incubation
for quite sometime

the poet encounters
tumult of hostile arena
cynical nihilistic platitudes
on redundanceof poetry

poet is unfazed
to portray the azure sky
sprinkling seven colours
of rainbow
add Beethoven's symphony
to the lilting
voice of cuckoo

accept the humility
of shrubs damped by dew
like demure

bride's eyelashes
having visitations
of butterflies
and vignettes
of floral mosaic

the murmurous melody
of the cool fountain
flowing down briskly
reminds the poet
of the flow of time
unrelenting ungrudging
only doling out
coolness plenitude, patience

signifying relationship
of effect with cause
end with means
finding words galore
amid pregnant silence
and impenetrable sighs
of the inane universe.

Somersault

Sizzling swelter
of summer
piercing blister
of ruthless sun
rising mercury around

political heat from
blaring microphones
road shows campaigns
by garlanded demagogues
with usual innuendoes
digs potshots
driving the thinking minds
into a boiling cauldron
of rattle and confusion

the thirsty doggie
enjoying siesta
blissfully
on a mound of sand
in reckless abandon
and gay procrastination

cute butterfly unfolding
the rainbow of myriad colours

prophesying uncertainty
of hung house
at the hustings

soiled statues
of erstwhile
unsung heroes
grinning and mocking at
the fake promises

that are doled out
copiously eloquently
like a mirage
in the desert
like a spell
of dry thunder
arousing vain hope of rain
for drought stricken peasants
like the expectant looks
of erotic stutues of kanark
waiting for fantasized lovers.

Forlorn House

Amid the depth
of growing dark night
the shrubs around the
ramshackle house
stand like a saint
spreading matted hair
anointing whole body
with oil of moss layers
breathing like a
hissing cobra

onlookers are intrigued
as to how
the house is
smouldered
each moment
burying
mysterious stillness
under its shallow foundation
till next dawn

morning sky sulks
with demure eyes
of a bride

wearing apron
of smoke
to hide shame

house has withstood
ravages of Time
like chronicles
of history
bruises on skin
speak volumes
casual flutter of birds
rattles it with
unknown panic
lest the remains
should lose identity

unwanted entry
of sun moon
on gaping holes
of chest
pierces into
distant past
like a sharp dagger
to retrieve
past cacophony

idle wind knocks on door
awaiting invitation
for entry inside

often thunder attempts
to break meditation
of saint like house
cloud bursts shouting

shook your sulk
shed your lust
old house
how long shall you
stand dejected ?
come join
sacred journey
into heaven
for that is
the truth ultimate.

Mother Land

India, Bharat, Hindustan
how sweet
pleasant aromatic
the fragrance
of its pluralism
multi-cultural backdrop
religious diversity
resonate across the globe

Greeks Persians Moguls Britons
have failed to maul
Indian vedic legacy
World Family concept
the concept of
"Vasudhaiva Kutumbakam"

devastating world wars
natural calamities
hardly succeed
to rattle Indian
social ethos
rather they
contribute to
strengthen
the bond of unity

and fraternity
amid diversity

since the auspicious day
India awoke
to freedom
when the whole
world was asleep
the D day
15 th August 1947
got off for
celebration
with patriotic fervour

its incessant struggle
is onto bring about
South Asian amity
to accelerate
global harmony

iconic epics
The Ramayan
The Mahabharat
are focus of research
in western states
Gandhi's policy
of truth nonviolence
is adored across the world

independence
through nonviolence
still intrigues
the western scholars

from Kashmir
to Kanyakumari
we are one
irrespective of diverse
cultures languages
castes religions

apparently a myth
or a miracle
but it is vividly palpable
very much entrenched
in our blood

Our fast industrial progress
nuclear experiments
appear to cause envy
among hostile neighbours

their malicious designs
to distort distintegrate
Indian unity
promoting Maoism
terrorism fundamentalism
nipped in the bud

all Indians imbibe patriotism'
holding Indian culture
as mainstay
they stand united
under the tricoloured Flag
to proudly
sing " Sare JahanseAchha
Hindu Sita Hamara".

Open Vault Pandora's

Relentless effort
made day in day out
no respite no work
no responsibility
no accountability

showing priority to
treasure hunt
after playing
icebreakers
we formed groups

what group?
not among
the strangers
among our own kin

since when our kin
no not exactly kin,
no one is kin here
but buddies
it's okay

society teaches us
harmony camaraderie
journey is on
voyage is on the sail
no albatross around
still juggernaut obstructed

wind hostile
ominous sound heard
nothing to do except
wait for inevitable to happen

this is the time
to reflect
to renege
to reminisce

fleeting glimpse
come slowly
letting loose
the pandora's vault
sealed so tightly

once out means
no matter
how when or where
you slowly came
caressed me
kissed me
but vanished like

mysterious
la belle dame
like morning dews in sun

since then
my hunt is on
haunted by
nightmares
scary visions
stayed undeterred
refused to give in
kept the quest on .

Smooth Passage

As I stretch my body
lying lazily
on the morning bed
a sight stirred me
my emotions
my heart

autumn perhaps
has sneaked in
like an unwanted guest

bunches of gulmohar
have disappeared
branches look pale
tree looks
weather-beaten
a few grey leaves
clinging unsurely
lost in
deep thought
as it were
when to leave

we don't say
one should not leave

leaving is the stark truth
as true as morning sun
or evening receding sun
receding into
hazy horizon
being unsure
if to come again

humans are like
the flies to
the wanton boys
but flies are
killed sparingly

it's done turn by turn
for some it is early
for some it is late
but each one's
turn comes

when we know
exit is inevitable
why regret
why lament
embrace it
gracefully
that will make you
free from angst
help make
a smooth passage.

In the Abyss

Submerged in the whirlpool
of labyrinthine depth
fathomless abyss

Man forgets values
main purpose
remains surrounded
by illusion of
material pursuits

objectives of birth
in this universe
scuttled blissfully
shares space
with own kin
own fraternity
with opacity diplomacy

trees shrubs plants
animals insects
differ with him
ignores dictates of
conscience alter ego

always carried away by
envy hatred
usual rat race
flaunts bloated ego
of being modern civilized

it's a misnomer perhaps
to view humans
as civilized
do they deserve it ?
are they worth the salt

creator's plan nullified
road map distorted
Satan sneaked in
Adam plucked
forbidden fruit
it is all chaos
Cain killed Abel
unleashing
primordial envy
culminating bloodshed

Man lost in
the labyrinth
fails to strike balance
among sattwa tama raja
stubbornly sidelines
tat-twam-asi

craze for
pelf power
position wealth

weave illusion
cobweb of surrealism
blinding him about
existential issues
food cloth shelter

about absolute truth
six feet land
six bamboos
at the end of life
without any
clue of salvation
or rebirth
in what form
real mystery
hard to unravel.

Mood swing

Haunted regularly
with riddles
debates dilemmas
shattered and helpless

a rudderless ship
indeed I am
don't know
can't even
conceive anything
nothing is clear

disturbed with
unresolved issues
never thought
anticipated
such a stage

tears well up
in my eyes
looking for reply
to contentious issues

but time unrelenting
laughs at me
pigeon on the
overturned tree
remains visible
reminding
many an event

charming cadence
of magical flute
comes floating
across Yamuna's
blue water

causing numerous ripples
across my nerves
why only me
girls dipped
in deep romance
feel happy
with unique thrill
love union
cherished since long
may turn dream
into real
for which
they waited
anxiously with
bated breath
since acons

waiting period
ending abruptly
ushers an aura
of redolent breeze
blowing on
sylvan landscape
my issues
riddles dilemma
blown away by
mood swing
in mainstream.

Phantom Unsalvageable

Endless wait
hovers around
half narrated story
half watched play
letter without address
and... words... feelings
dumped in oblivion
amid fathomless abyss

vast stretch of
time with angst anxiety
regret remorse reflections
begin to grope
oscillate between
hope hopelessness

will the wait be over
fatigue restlessness
hang heavy
as it happens
with traveller

making journey
without destination

hope sustains
nurses grudge
for lack of fulfillment

accomplishment
success victory
are all myths

Sisyphean strife
apparently fulfilling
illusory at the long last
irritating unending agonizing
that stretches into eternity

death may heal it
who knows
in what way
regret of wait
unfulfilled desire
insulting failure
in rat race
shall always haunt
like a phantom
whose soul not salvaged
for wrong rituals.

Not a Human indeed

Not a human as yet
it's doubtful
if we know
human qualities
attributes virtues
doubt is well founded

turn over pages
of news papers
hordes of rapes murders
loots arson cyber fraud
make headlines
compassion tolerance sacrifice
take back seat
like bad money
driving good money
out of circulation

corruption becomes
hallmark of bureaucracy
mind's horse gallops
speedily but proves futile

it goes wrong way
sometimes we feel
independence acquired
through hard labour
appears a slur

colonialism was better
noticeable change
occurred after
independence
same class distinction
women marginalization
racial strife fraud pretence

sun rises every morning
but hardly brings new dawn
fed up with stereotypes
don't know when new sun
shall usher new era.

Till the End

We forget quite often
what are our basic
requirements
perhaps a handful of rice
a piece of cloth
a modest roof
over our head
once we solve
existential issues
we are free
to do anything and everything

but no
the braided cotton wick
dipped in the oil of wants
lit with
the flame of ambition
is made to burn
without interruption

brake of conscience
fails to control speed
fuelled by competition
unfair unhealthy

wife's tantrums
friend's leg pulling
neighbour's wealth
although ill got
causes envy
prompts to stray
from untrodden path
take to the most
trodden one
with apparent dead grass
that help boost fledgling
undeserving people
prosper overnight
like the wild shrubs
in uncut forest

feel tired
joining rat race
of vain status
fake position
how long
shall it go on
perhaps till end of life.

No Escape

Who asked you
not to dream?
dreams are birds
sitting on tree
playing hide and seek
with darkness
masked under
a black cloth

some one
stands in front
beckons slowly
with crooked smile
says your time is off
tread on reality
dream is short
make-believe world
always misleading
brittle illusory

when dream
is broken
you realize
the truth
flowers are odourless
surrounding is colourless
body is fragile powerless
scared by unknown fear
stunned to survey
circle is about to complete

so why delay ?
be ready to face
embrace the inevitable
no escape from it.

Sylvan Dream

It feels like
the other day
was it special ?
of course very special

aeons have passed
not touched the contours
nor did it stave off

infact it is
immortal real
physical or fantasy
irrespective of shape
feeling is sublime
beach was snow white
moon in a state of blush

you too were reserve
hiatus deepened
pain hurtful
zinx is to be addressed
initiation made
response came positive
lying indolently

on my sprawling lap
you spoke to moon
moon also spoke

I kept mum
you said
waves are infectious
your company
is rare mystical magical

insecurity gripped you
lest someone should
steal precious gem
magical company
from your kitty

solace came
after my strong promise
to stick to you life long
like a shadow

moon is in my kitty
you said
slipped into
a state of dream
soothing serene
sylvan sublime.

Not for Sharing

Bestial game
heinous conspiracy
unlimited hatred
inconceivable envy

habitat is polluted
making life risky
causing asphyxiation
suffocation
know not
what type of oxygen
shall bring relief

world with water colour
visible from far off space
adjacent to
sprawling horizon
looks over
in a gesture
of amen,
let it be

where am I ?
I have never thought
may be unconcerned

turned a stoic
aware of helplessness
shorn of powers
human superhuman
supramental
get resigned to fate
what cannot be cured
must be endured

in a still state
of meditation
quietness practice
much touted
life's lullaby
like consoling
infantile obstinacy
with pack of kinder joy

counting on remote
anxiety ridden
consolation
I grope for
exploring right path
as a misguided tourist

such a plight is
undoubtedly amazing
as it were but alas
it can be felt
at heart's core
not meant for sharing.

What was Feared

Amid fathomless vacuum
divine desire descended
demon divine rift
widened day by day

yawning the worry
all around
peace lost
plenitude a thing of past
only remained conflict

how to resolve
keep both sides cool
restore past harmony
not exactly past harmony
but at least semblance of it

fire cannot restrain
its hunger
to burn the inflammable
not that solution
is beyond reach
what is needed

is willpower
to draw road map
for solution

happened actually
the day cherishable
memorable to indulge
in lavishing
pampering passion
incredible ecstasy

reason is such
humans evolved
to catalyze
demon divine conflict

humans with Manu Satarupa
as primordial parents
made sincere efforts
to build up citadel
of civilization on
rubric of
discipline morality
never thought
humans to indecently
conduct as demons
alas ! that happened
what was feared.

Meaningful Sojourn

Someone rightly said
hypocrisy stalks everywhere
clubinox multiplex
mall hotel resort
roadside eatery
and also there
where one cannot imagine

there in my granny's betel box
in grandpa's bookshelf
studded with BhagvadGeeta
Kathopanishad Isavasya Upanishad
Brihadaranyak Upanishad
preserving morals scruples
dos don'ts ethics
undoablesattainablesuntenables
Nachiket's interaction
with God of Death
on self knowledge
acquisition of Agnividya
Dutta Dayadwam Damyata

YamaRaj's explanation
on Preya and Shreya
materialism and spiritualism
the essence of the soul

human soul's link
emergence evolution
any one knows little
nor is there
any interest
to dive into
the tapestry of spiritualism
to traverse the mysterious
trajectory of life's
arduous journey

youth beauty wealth
ofter temporal pleasure
real pleasure lasts longer
that is eternal perennial

it is hard to say
when we will realize
this supramental truth
wake up from slumber
to make this earthly sojourn
more meaningful.

Fly wings Fly

Fatigue ridden wings
how long shall
help me fly
nothing to worry
flew a lot
ineredible distance covered
unbelievable speed
bewitching scenery
picturesque landscapes
multi-coloured butterflies

floating clouds gave
motivation to fly
till eternity
but it's not possible
if anything any process
starts has to
end somewhere
windup albeit
with utter reluctance

not me everyone
is like that
unbridled greed

insatiable thirst
never ending wants
haunt us all
Adam or Prometheus
who so ever
is the primordial father
enlivening the myth
is a source of eternal
suffering of progeny

perpetuation of
progenital sin
never stops
generates
multipronged misery

soaring flight
in the wings of imagination
is considered the panacea
to rid the curse
absolve of the sin

wake up wings!
never tire out
fly soar above
sky is your limit.

Siren

Listen to your conscience
now a days a rare thing
impulse predominates
no patience to ponder
conclusion comes instantly

major reason
why many mistakes
afflict society
any attempt to avoid
overcome or wriggle out
ends in fiasco

rescue measures
are untenable
a moment's folly
bring despair
for centuries

conscience alter ego super ego
guide you properly
only thing is to
obey guidance
guidance based

on objectivity
is always welcome

there is no bias
no partiality
no nepotism
major miseries
turmoil's chaos
occur for biased
impulsive action
like Othello
getting so convinced
by Iago's malicious move
as to go to the fatal extent
of strangulating Desdemona

innocent life sacrificed
on the altar of impulse
blinded vengeance
based on credulity

never ever trust blindly
take all care to examine
verify the veracity
may be allegation
or adulation
take care
observe caution
or else doomsday
will blow siren.

Deep Dive

Moon of Bhadrav sky
especially on
the second night
winks at me
tickles my senses

I blabber out
chandrika come come
you know how
time is fleeting

be serious
feel my love
my emotions feelings
kept fresh untouched
unravished in
my heart's garden

I never allow any wasp
any butterfly
to have its maiden taste
It's like the Prasad
offered to the Almighty
with proper care caution
devotion feeling of surrender

my love is twenty four
carat gold
sans any dross
rain soaked soil
watery leaves of grass
make me see your
wet eyelashes
after mild fight

it is you know
remains short lived
my lips stealthily proceed
to caress your forehead face
such surreptitious adventures
lift your forlorn spirit
to the haven of joy
your stread effort
to keep me under clutches
pays dividend

Chandrika understand
time's importance
once gone never returns
so why dilly dallying
before time runs out
let us have deep dive
in the ocean of love
with whale's zeal.

River Daya's Saga

While going down
the memory lane
browsing the dog eared yellow
pages of my diary
I am struck with awe
and wonder to notice
some notes on the colour of water

what colour?
does water have any colour
normally water is said
to have no colour
if it is having any
may come under
white category

milk is white in colour
water colour hardly matches it
but river Daya's water
the historic water
legendaryDaya's water
receives iconic status
during kalinga war

a nation Kalinga
the land of courage
conviction dedication patriotism
fleet of warriors
cared not for death
showed commendable skill
in leadership albeit king
did not lead the fleet

fierce battle brought
valiant emperor
of Mauryan dynasty
on his toes
was stunned flabbergasted
to see the invincible courage
dauntless dedication

Ashok although victor
accepted moral defeat
laid down his arms
said Buddham Saranam gachhami
Dharmam Saranam gachhami
Sangham Saranam gachhami
Daya narrates the saga.

BLACK EAGLE BOOKS

www.blackeaglebooks.org
info@blackeaglebooks.org

Black Eagle Books, an independent publisher, was founded as a nonprofit organization in April, 2019. It is our mission to connect and engage the Indian diaspora and the world at large with the best of works of world literature published on a collaborative platform, with special emphasis on foregrounding Contemporary Classics and New Writing.

www.ingramcontent.com/pod-product-compliance
Lightning Source LLC
Chambersburg PA
CBHW060615080526
44585CB00013B/840